Enough
Living Your Life in the Right Measure

by Melinda Haynes

Copyright © 2026 by Melinda Haynes
All rights reserved.

No part of this publication may be reproduced, distributed, or transmitted in any form or by any means—including photocopying, recording, or other electronic or mechanical methods—without prior written permission from the author, except for brief quotations used in reviews, articles, or scholarly works.

This is a work of nonfiction based on the author's personal experience and professional insights. It is intended for inspirational and educational purposes and is not a substitute for professional therapy or medical advice.

Cover art and interior design by Melinda Haynes.

ISBN: 979-8-9990654-2-1
First Edition – 2026
Published by Harbor & Quill Publishing
www.HarborQuill.com
Author: www.MelindaHaynes.com

Dedication

To the One who never asked me to carry what wasn't mine,
and patiently taught me the difference.

To those who learned to survive by holding everything together —
may you discover the relief of putting the burden down.

To those who have been the strong one for far too long —
may these pages remind you that peace awaits.

Acknowledgements

To my clients, interns, and readers—your willingness to face what is difficult, and to question what you have been carrying, continues to teach me more than you know. This book is for you.

To Jen — thank you for being the "fun aunt." Your strength and success have always been a positive example for me, and your quiet, steady encouragement has sustained me.

With gratitude,
Melinda

Table of Contents

Introduction 1
Chapter One: You're Not Wrong 3
Chapter Two: Why Enough Is So Hard to Recognize 7
Chapter Three: Sufficiency 9
Chapter Four: Readiness 13
Chapter Five: Limits 17
Chapter Six: Endings 21
Chapter Seven: Authority 25
Chapter Eight: Living with Enough 29
About the Author 32

Enough: Living Your Life in the Right Measure

Introduction

Most people don't arrive at a book like this because they are careless, lazy, or unwilling to grow. They arrive because something that once worked no longer does.

At some point, effort stops producing clarity. Endurance stops bringing peace. The strategies that once helped you survive begin to feel heavy, even when nothing obvious has gone wrong. You may still be functioning well. You may still be responsible, capable, and dependable. And yet, something feels off—like you are carrying more than is actually required.

Often, the trouble is not that you haven't done enough.

It's that you've done more than was ever yours to do.

Many of us were taught—explicitly or implicitly—that stopping is a failure, that limits are selfish, that rest must be earned, and that love is proven by how much we are willing to tolerate.

Over time, those beliefs become habits. We keep going. We keep explaining. We keep fixing. We keep holding things together long after they have reached their natural end.

Not because we are foolish. But because we were never taught how to recognize when something is complete.

The word *enough* tends to feel loaded. For some, it sounds like giving up. For others, it feels unsafe, premature, or unkind. Many people associate it with scarcity or resignation. But that is not how it is used here.

In this book, *enough* is not about doing less for the sake of restraint. It is about learning to see clearly. It is about proportion, discernment, and authority—the ability to recognize when something has reached its rightful measure and to let that recognition guide your next step.

This is not a book about fixing yourself. It is not a book about becoming more disciplined, more resilient, or more tolerant.

It is a book about judgment—quiet, grounded judgment. The kind that allows you to stop without guilt, to continue without fear, and to rest without apology.

If you are reading this because you feel tired of second-guessing yourself…
If you sense that some part of your life is asking for a different kind of attention…
If you are beginning to wonder whether peace might come not from doing more, but from doing what is actually yours—

You are in the right place.

Chapter One: You're Not Wrong

This book is not meant to be rushed. If you've arrived here feeling tired, uncertain, or quietly overwhelmed, pause for a moment. Take a breath. Let yourself notice where you are. Nothing needs to be solved yet.

Enough is not a manual, a checklist, or a set of techniques to master. It is a framework for wise discretion—a way of learning how to recognize when something has reached its rightful measure. Because of that, how you read this book matters as much as what it says.

You do not need to apply everything at once. You do not need to reach a conclusion by the final page. The purpose of this book is not to tell you what to do, but to help you notice what you are already doing—and whether it is still necessary for peaceful living.

There is often a quiet relief in realizing this. A sense of being seen. Of discovering that the strain you've been carrying has context, and that you are not wrong for feeling it.

Read Slowly, Not Strategically: This is a short book by design. Its usefulness comes from attention, not volume. You may notice the impulse to read quickly in order to "get it" or move on to application. If that happens, pause. Speed is often a sign that we are looking for resolution rather than understanding.

Let the ideas settle before you decide what they mean for you. Some readers find it helpful to read one chapter at a time, with space in between.

Others prefer to read the book straight through and return later to the chapters that linger. There is no correct approach—only an honest one.

Notice What Stands Out—and What Doesn't: Not every chapter will land the same way. Some sections may feel obvious. Others may feel unsettling. Pay attention to which ideas provoke resistance, defensiveness, or discomfort. Those reactions often indicate places where you have been carrying more than is required—or postponing a decision you already sense needs to be made.

At the same time, notice what feels quietly relieving. Relief is often a signal that something true has been named. You are not required to act on every insight. Recognition alone can begin to restore proportion.

Use the Chapters as Lenses, Not Rules: Each chapter addresses a different judgment related to enough: sufficiency, readiness, limits, completion, and authority. These are not stages to complete or boxes to check. They are lenses to which you can return as needed.

At different times, different judgments will matter more. You may find yourself rereading one chapter repeatedly while others fade into the background. That is evidence that discernment is contextual. Enough is always specific to the moment.

Resist the Urge to Over-Apply: It may be tempting to use this book to evaluate other people—to decide where they are doing too much, where they should stop, where they are misjudging "enough."

If that impulse arises, notice it, then gently return to yourself. This book is most useful when applied inwardly. Its purpose is not to help you manage others more, but to clarify your own responsibility. Proportion begins there.

Let Decisions Emerge, Rather Than Be Forced: You may finish this book without a clear action step—and that is okay. Some decisions surface immediately. Others require time. This book is meant to change how you see, not to pressure you into premature movement.

When a decision is ready, it will first emerge, then feel simpler than you expect. Not necessarily easier—but cleaner. Less entangled. More settled. Trust that timing.

Return When You Need To: *Enough* is not a one-time read. Many readers return to it when they feel overextended, uncertain, or stuck in unnecessary effort. Others revisit it during transitions, endings, or decisions that feel heavier than they should.

You do not need to remember every concept. You only need to become more aware of when something feels like too much—or when something is already complete.

This book is meant to be a companion, not a conclusion.

A Final Note Before We Dig In: If at any point while reading you find yourself thinking, " This feels too simple," you are not missing something.

Simplicity is often what remains after excess has been removed. And sometimes, simplicity is exactly what we need.

If you've felt even a slight easing while reading—an exhale, a sense of being understood—let that be enough for now. That, too, is a sign that help has already begun to arrive.

Melinda Haynes

Chapter Two: Why Enough Is So Hard to Recognize

Most of us don't struggle because we lack effort, insight, or care. We struggle because we don't know when to stop.

We live in a culture that rewards more—more availability, more explanation, more endurance, more success, more compliance—often without asking whether any of it is still required. The assumption is simple and rarely questioned: if something is good, more of it must be better.

If a little effort helps, more effort must heal. If staying longer once helped, staying indefinitely must be loving. If holding on once prevented loss, holding on tighter must be faithfulness.

And yet, many people find themselves exhausted not because they haven't done enough, but because they have done far more than was ever theirs to do.

At some point, the problem stops being willingness and becomes judgment.

This book is not about motivation.
It is not about healing techniques.
It is not about learning to tolerate more.

It is about learning to recognize when something is enough—not as a feeling, but as a decision.

Most of the distress we experience in adult life can be traced back to one quiet uncertainty: *Am I enough?*

When that question goes unanswered, we default to excess. We over-extend, over-explain, over-function, over-give, and overstay—not because we are weak, but because we are unsure where the line actually is.

We confuse persistence with wisdom.
Endurance with virtue.
Availability with love.
Enough is the word that interrupts that confusion.

It is a small word, but it carries authority. It appears when something has reached its proper measure. When a task is complete. When a limit has been met. When a decision no longer needs revisiting. When continuation would add strain rather than meaning.

Enough is not a rejection.
It is not indifference.
It is not withdrawal.
It is discernment.

Peace tends to arrive—not when everything is fixed—but when what is not required is finally set down. Calm appears when responsibility is rightly sized. Rest becomes possible when the work that belongs to us is distinguished from the work that does not.

This book will not tell you exactly where your *enough* is or "should" be. That judgment cannot be outsourced.

Instead, it will walk you through the places where enough is most often misjudged—where we assume more is needed when it is not, where we continue past the natural conclusion, where we hesitate to claim authority over our own stopping point.

Enough is not something you achieve.
It is something you learn to recognize.
And when you do, life does not become smaller.
It becomes manageable.
This is what it means to live life in the right measure.

Welcome to *Enough*.

Chapter Three: Sufficiency

Most people assume they struggle because something is missing. They need...
More clarity.
More healing.
More effort.
More faith.
More time.

Sufficiency challenges that assumption.

Sufficiency is not the belief that everything is abundant or easy. It is the judgment that what is required for this moment is already present.

Not ideal.
Not perfect.
Simply adequate.

We tend to overlook sufficiency because it lacks drama. It does not announce itself loudly. It does not create urgency. In fact, sufficiency often feels quiet enough that we mistrust it. We assume that if something truly mattered, it would feel more pressing—more demanding of our attention.

So we keep adding.

We add explanations when silence would have been sufficient.
We add effort when competence was already present.
We add responsibility when the task had already been completed.

Over time, this habit trains us to live as if lack is the default—even when it isn't.

Sufficiency asks a different question.

Not *What more is needed?*
But *What is already here that I'm overlooking?*

This question can feel unsettling at first. If nothing is missing, then the reason for our continued striving begins to dissolve. And with it, the justification for carrying more than is required.

Many people resist sufficiency because they confuse it with complacency. They worry that if they admit something is sufficient, growth will stop. Progress will stall. Meaning will fade.

But sufficiency does not end movement.
It ends unnecessary movement.
It does not deny improvement.
It restores proportion.

A parent who has provided enough care does not need to keep proving their devotion through exhaustion. A leader who has given clear direction does not need to hover. A person who has spoken truthfully does not need to keep rephrasing themselves in hopes of a different response.
At some point, the task had already been done.

An Example of Enough
The decision was stated. Anna had sent the email. The explanation was complete the first time she hit "send." Nothing essential had been missing. And still, she opened the email again.

She reread what she'd written, scanning for places it might land too sharply or invite confusion. She considered making adjustments, adding a qualifier, softening a phrase.

Not because anything she had written was unclear—but because not reflecting felt exposed. Vulnerable. Cursory.

She told herself she was being careful. Thoughtful. Responsible.

But as she re-read and worried, a familiar fatigue settled in. Not the tiredness that comes from effort, but the heavier kind that comes from continuation. The sense that she was still tending to something that no longer required her attention. Time being wasted.

She stared at the screen. Nothing new came to mind. No additional clarity. No truth she hadn't already said. Only the quiet realization that anything she added now would not change the outcome—only prolong her involvement.

The email was already enough. Closing the document felt uncomfortable, as though she were leaving something unfinished. But nothing was unfinished. The discomfort came from allowing adequacy to stand without reinforcement.

She shut the laptop anyway. Not because everything felt resolved—but because, for once, she allowed what was sufficient to remain so.

Sufficiency is not laziness.
It is restraint.
And restraint is a form of wisdom.

When sufficiency is misjudged, people begin to live as though everything is fragile. As though relationships will collapse without constant effort. As though worth must be continually reinforced. As though rest is earned only after depletion.

But when sufficiency is rightly recognized, something steadies.
You begin to notice when your energy is being spent not because it is required, but because it feels safer to keep going than to stop. You begin to see how often *just in case* has replaced discernment. You begin to recognize how much labor you've been doing to compensate for a lack that may not actually exist.

Sufficiency does not ask you to convince yourself that you are whole.
It asks you to tell the truth about what is already present.
And truth has a quiet way of reducing excess.

This is often where peace begins—not because life has been solved, but because the question has changed. You are no longer asking how to add more, but how to honor what is already enough.

Living your life in the right measure starts here—with the willingness to consider that you may not be lacking what you think you are.

Chapter Four: Readiness

Many people confuse readiness with confidence. They wait to feel certain before they act.
Prepared before they decide. Calm before they speak. Fully resolved before they move forward. When those feelings don't arrive, they assume the answer must be *not yet*.

So they wait.

Readiness, however, is not an emotional state.
It is a judgment.
It is the discernment that something is adequate for its purpose—not ideal, not complete, not guaranteed to succeed, but sufficient for what is being asked now.

We often delay because we are looking for assurance when what we actually need is clarity.
Readiness asks a quieter question than confidence ever does:
Is this enough for this moment?
Not forever.
Not for every outcome.
Not for every possible response.
Just for what is required now.

When readiness is misjudged, people tend to swing between two extremes. Some take on responsibility prematurely, assuming they should already be capable of what they have not yet grown into. Others postpone action indefinitely, mistaking hesitation for wisdom and fear for discernment.

Both positions are rooted in the same confusion: the belief that readiness must be absolute rather than contextual.

But adequacy is always relative to purpose. A person can be ready to speak honestly without being ready to be understood. Ready to begin without being ready to finish. Ready to try without being ready to master.

When we demand more readiness than the moment requires, we turn discernment into delay. We begin to treat responsibility as something that must be perfectly matched to outcome rather than appropriately matched to effort.

This is how people stay over-prepared and under-present.

They rehearse conversations that never happen.
They refine plans that never move forward.
They wait for clarity that can only be gained by acting.
At some point, the opportunity has already arrived—or worse, left.

An Example of Enough
Rick had been considering the decision for months. He'd read about it. Talked it through with people he trusted. Made lists—pros and cons, risks and contingencies. He prepared the proper documents and thought through every possible outcome.
Each time he came close to moving forward, he found another reason to wait. Another angle to consider. Another variable that needed to be addressed first.

He told himself he was being responsible. But beneath the preparation was something harder to admit: he wanted certainty. Not just that the decision was reasonable, but that it would turn out well. That it would be affirmed. That he wouldn't regret it.

The moment itself was simple. A conversation he needed to initiate. A step that did not require mastery, only honesty. He was not being asked to resolve everything—only to begin.

Still, he hesitated.

He noticed the cost not in catastrophe, but in stagnation. The low-grade restlessness that came from circling the same decision without engaging it. The sense that life was happening adjacent to him, while he remained in preparation mode.

Nothing new had been learned in years. No additional clarity had emerged. The delay was no longer serving discernment—it was protecting him from exposure. From vulnerability.

What he already knew and already had was enough to start.

Readiness does not mean you will not struggle.
It does not mean you will have everything figure out.
It does not mean you won't feel awkward.
It means you are adequately equipped to begin.
To take the first step in a new direction.

There is a particular kind of exhaustion that comes from refusing to acknowledge readiness. It shows up as second-guessing, restlessness, and a feeling of being perpetually behind or left out. Life begins to feel like something you are hoping for rather than participating in.

Often, this exhaustion has less to do with capacity and more to do with reluctance to accept that enough preparation has already occurred.

Readiness requires honesty. It requires acknowledging when the reason you are waiting is not because something is missing, but because you are afraid of what will be revealed once you begin.

Starting has a way of exposing limits, outcomes, and reactions that perpetual preparation keeps at bay. But postponing action does not protect you from those realities. It only delays your encounter with them.

Readiness is not a promise of success. It is permission to engage. And engagement, when rightly measured, is rarely reckless.

It is bounded.
Responsive.
Open to correction.

It allows for learning. It allows for stopping, if stopping becomes necessary.

People who live without a sense of readiness tend to overextend in some areas while restraining themselves in others. They give too much where they feel obligated and too little where they feel uncertain. Life becomes uneven—not because they lack ability, but because they have lost trust in their own discernment.

Recognizing readiness restores proportion. You begin to say "yes" where participation is appropriate, and "no" where delay has become avoidance. You stop requiring yourself to be more prepared than the situation warrants. You accept that adequacy, not perfection, is what most moments actually require.

Readiness does not remove risk. It places risk in the right measure. When readiness is rightly judged, movement becomes simpler. Decisions become cleaner. The constant internal negotiation quiets.

You no longer need to ask whether you are fully prepared—only whether what you have is sufficient for what is being asked. And often, it is.

This is not a call to push yourself prematurely.
It is an invitation to stop underestimating what you already carry.

Living your life in the right measure means knowing when preparation has done its work—and when it is time to step forward with what is already enough.

Chapter Five: Limits

Most people don't struggle with limits because they don't care. They struggle because limits feel like refusal—of love, of responsibility, of growth, of goodness itself. Saying *no more* can feel like a moral failure rather than an act of discernment.

So instead of setting limits, people negotiate with themselves.
They stretch a little longer.
They explain one more time.
They stay available just in case.

Limits get postponed not because they are unclear, but because they feel costly.
Limits, however, are not acts of rejection. They are judgments of measure. A limit marks the point at which continuation no longer serves what it was meant to protect. It is the recognition that more effort will not produce more fruit—only more strain.

When limits are misjudged, excess becomes normalized. Overextension starts to feel like devotion. Endurance becomes a stand-in for wisdom. People confuse staying longer with caring more.

But limits are not about caring less. They are about knowing when caring has done its work.

Every healthy system has limits. Bodies, seasons, relationships, institutions—all function within bounds. Without limits, systems don't become more loving or effective. They become unstable.

The same is true for people. A person without limits does not become generous. They become depleted.

Limits are often avoided because they feel abrupt. Final. Unkind. But most limits are not sudden. They are delayed acknowledgments of something that has been true for a long time.

The moment you say "I've had enough" is rarely the moment *enough* actually occurred. It is simply the moment you stopped ignoring it.

This is why limits can feel uncomfortable even when they are necessary. They force alignment between reality and action. They end the internal dissonance of knowing something is too much while continuing anyway.

An Example of Enough
For a long time, Claire believed that being unconditionally available was part of being faithful—to her role, to her relationships, to her sense of self. When someone needed her, she responded. When something went unfinished, she stepped in. When expectations blurred, she absorbed the extra weight, usually without complaint.

She told herself she was being supportive. But over time, the cost became harder to ignore. Not in dramatic ways—no breaking point, no confrontation—but in subtler ones. A constant low-grade irritability. A sense of quiet resentment she didn't recognize as such. Fatigue that rest didn't seem to resolve.

What troubled her most was that she couldn't point to a single moment where things had gone wrong. Nothing she was doing felt unreasonable in isolation. It was the accumulation that was wearing her down.

One evening, she noticed herself rereading a message she hadn't yet answered. The request was familiar. The expectation was unspoken but implied. She knew exactly what she would say if she responded—"Sure, no problem," because that is what she always said.
And for the first time, she noticed something else.
The limit had already been reached.
Not just that evening.
Not just that week.
But long before.

She had crossed it gradually, without naming it, and had been compensating ever since.

Responding now would not simply preserve the relationship. It would preserve the pattern. The discomfort she felt wasn't about setting a boundary; it was about the potential consequences. Would she feel guilty for saying, "I'm available then," or "Sorry, not this time"? Would her friend be upset with her?

Many people fear that setting a limit will escalate conflict. Sometimes it does. But more often, what escalates conflict is the absence of clear limits. Ambiguity creates room for resentment, confusion, and misplaced responsibility.

A clear limit may disappoint someone.
An unclear limit will exhaust everyone.

Limits do not require explanation to be valid. They do not need consensus to be legitimate. They do not need to be justified by extreme circumstances to be wise.

They simply need to be true.

One of the most difficult parts of learning limits is accepting that other people may disagree with where you draw them. They may push back. They may reinterpret your restraint as withdrawal or punishment.

But limits are not about managing reactions. They are about honoring reality. When you refuse to acknowledge limits, you end up compensating for them in other ways. You become irritable instead of clear. Distant instead of direct. Over-functioning instead of boundaried.

Limits, when named early, prevent those distortions. They preserve relationship by preserving proportion. A limit says: *this is where my responsibility ends*. It does not say that you don't care what happens next. It says that what happens next is no longer yours to carry.

This distinction is subtle but essential. People who live without limits often believe they are being selfless. In reality, they are avoiding the discomfort of stopping. They are postponing a decision that only they can make. Limits return that authority.

Limits allow you to participate fully where participation is appropriate—and to step back where it is not. They keep effort aligned with purpose. They offer protection from misdirected responsibility, unnecessary strain, and depletion.

Living your life in the right measure requires the courage to stop when stopping is the wise thing to do. Not because you are done caring. But because caring has reached its proper boundary.
And beyond that point, more is no longer required.

Chapter Six: Endings

Many people struggle to finish a task, chore, project, or relationship. Not because they are careless or uncommitted, but because fulfillment feels ambiguous. Ending something well often lacks the clarity of beginning it. There is no announcement. No external signal. No universal agreement that something is, in fact, done.

So people linger.
They revisit conversations that have already been had.
They continue refining work that has already met its purpose.
They stay emotionally engaged in situations that no longer require their presence.

The endings gets delayed because it can feel abrupt—even when it is appropriate.
Ending is not perfection.

It is the recognition that the requirement has been met.
This distinction matters more than we realize.

Perfection keeps people stuck. It demands certainty, polish, and immunity from regret. The ending asks something simpler: *Is anything essential still missing?* If the answer is no, the work is complete—even if the outcome is imperfect, even if the response is mixed, even if the ending is quiet.

When an ending is misjudged, effort continues past usefulness. People keep adjusting long after adjustments are meaningful. They keep showing up long after presence has become symbolic rather than necessary.

Over time, this produces a particular kind of fatigue—not from hard work, but from unnecessary continuation.

Endings require trust.

Trust that what has been offered is sufficient.
Trust that more input will not change the outcome.
Trust that leaving space does not mean abandoning responsibility.

Many people avoid endings because they confuse them with disengagement. They worry that ending something means they don't care anymore, that stopping means they failed, that closure implies indifference.

But endings are not always withdrawal. They are alignment. An ending aligns action with purpose. It honors the scope of responsibility rather than expanding it indefinitely. It allows effort to rest where it was meant to.

A completed task does not need defending.
A completed season does not need revisiting.
A completed contribution does not need constant reinforcement.

An Example of Enough
For months, Nathan had been revising the same project. Not because it was unfinished, but because he couldn't decide what *finished* meant. Each time he reviewed it, he found something small to improve. A phrase to adjust. A detail to clarify. Nothing substantial—just enough to justify another pass.

He told himself he was being thorough. But the revisions had stopped changing the work. They were only extending his involvement with it. The original purpose had been met long ago. What remained was his reluctance to release it without knowing how it would be received.

The project had moved beyond Nathan in every way except one: he hadn't allowed it to end. He noticed the cost in the background of his days. A low-level pressure, as though something was always waiting. A sense that he couldn't fully turn his attention elsewhere because this one thing was still open, still unresolved.

When he asked himself what was missing, nothing surfaced. No unmet requirement. No overlooked responsibility. Only the discomfort of letting the work stand without further adjustment.

Finality, an ending, he realized, wasn't asking him to be proud of the outcome. It was asking him to be honest about it. The work was done. Endings make room.

They create space for rest, for attention to shift, for something new to begin. Without endings, life becomes congested. Old responsibilities pile up alongside new ones. Nothing fully ends, so nothing new fully begins.

This is how people become busy without being effective, engaged without being present.
Finality is often resisted because it requires letting go of control. Once something is finished, it moves beyond your management. It enters the realm of response, consequence, and outcome—things you can influence but not control.

Continuing to tinker can feel safer than accepting that reality. But refusing an ending does not preserve influence. It erodes clarity.

A clear ending allows responsibility to return to its proper place. It signals that your role has been fulfilled and that what follows now belongs elsewhere.
This does not mean you cannot care about the outcome. It means you no longer carry it. An ending is a form of honesty. It tells the truth about what was asked and what was given. It acknowledges that effort has limits and that exceeding them does not add meaning.

It respects both the work and the worker.

When people learn to recognize the importance of endings, they stop dragging the past into the present. They stop reworking what has already served its purpose. They stop measuring worth by how long they stay involved.

Life begins to feel cleaner.
Not easier, necessarily—but clearer.

Living your life in the right measure means knowing when something has reached its end. Not rushing it. Not resisting it. Simply recognizing that the work is done. And allowing yourself to step forward without carrying what no longer requires your hands.

Chapter Seven: Authority

At some point, every question of *enough* comes down to authority. Not authority over others— but authority over decision.

Most people delay decisions not because they lack information, but because they are unsure whether they are *allowed* to decide. They wait for confirmation, consensus, or consequences extreme enough to justify stopping or limiting.

Until then, they remain suspended—continuing, explaining, accommodating—hoping the decision will eventually make itself. It rarely does.

Authority is the capacity to declare when something is enough and to live accordingly.

It is not forceful.
It is not loud.
It does not require agreement to be real.
It simply ends the deliberation.

Many people avoid authority because they associate it with dominance or control. They fear that claiming authority will make them rigid, selfish, or unkind. So they defer—assuming that if a decision truly mattered, someone else would make it clearer.

But authority does not emerge from clarity alone. It emerges from responsibility. If you are the one carrying the cost of continuation, you are the one responsible for deciding when it stops. Outsourcing that decision does not remove the cost—it only removes your agency. When authority is avoided, people live reactively. They adjust based on pressure rather than judgment. They say yes until exhaustion forces a no. They keep explaining in hopes that understanding will replace the need to decide.

But understanding rarely ends responsibility. Decision does. Authority does not mean you will always be right. It means you will no longer be paralyzed.

A decision can be revised.
Indecision compounds.

This is why authority is essential to proportion. Without it, even good instincts remain dormant. You may sense that something is sufficient, complete, or no longer required—but until you claim the authority to act on that judgment, nothing changes. Authority turns recognition into movement.

An Example of Enough
For a long time, Michael believed he was being flexible. When a situation became uncomfortable, he stayed. When expectations shifted, he adjusted. When something no longer felt sustainable, he looked for a way to endure it a little longer. He told himself he was being patient. Reasonable. Cooperative.

But over time, he noticed that the cost of staying never disappeared—it simply transferred. The longer he delayed deciding, the more tired he became. The more he explained, the less clear things felt. What he called flexibility was slowly turning into resentment.

The decision itself was not complex. He had known for a while what he needed to do. What kept him stuck was not confusion, but permission. He was waiting for circumstances to force his hand so that he wouldn't have to claim the choice as his own.

When he finally stopped explaining and made the decision quietly, something surprised him.
The relief did not come from the outcome. It came from the ownership. Nothing external had changed yet.

Reactions were still unknown. Consequences still uncertain. But the internal debate—the constant negotiation—had ended. The decision had been made.

Many people are more comfortable with obligation than authority. Obligation allows them to remain responsive without being decisive. Authority, by contrast, requires ownership. It acknowledges that you are choosing—not merely complying.

This can feel unsettling at first. Choosing means accepting that some people may disagree. That outcomes may not be ideal. That limiting or stopping does not guarantee relief for everyone involved.

But refusing authority does not prevent these realities—it simply prolongs them.

Authority is not about having the final word in every situation.
It is about having the rightful word in your own.
It allows you to say, *This is enough*, without apology.
It allows you to stop explaining decisions that are already sound.
It allows you to remain steady even when others push for more.

When authority is rightly exercised, something settles. The constant internal debate quiets. You are no longer negotiating with yourself at every turn. Effort aligns with judgment. Action follows discernment.

Peace does not come from perfect decisions. It comes from owned decisions. Living your life in the right measure requires accepting that no one else can decide *enough* for you.

Advice can inform.
Wisdom can guide.
Faith can anchor.
But the declaration itself belongs to you.

Authority is not the absence of care. It is the presence of responsibility. And when authority is claimed, *enough* no longer remains a question waiting to be answered. It becomes a decision that has been made.

Chapter Eight: Living with Enough

Living with enough is not about restraint for its own sake. It is about proportion. It is learning to recognize when something has reached its rightful measure—and allowing that recognition to guide your actions, rather than fear, habit, or a sense of obligation.

Enough is not discovered all at once. It is learned through repeated judgments—judgments about sufficiency, readiness, limits, completion, and authority. Over time, those judgments begin to shape how you move through the world.

You stop adding where nothing is missing.
You stop preparing where you are already ready.
You stop continuing where the work is complete.
You stop waiting for permission to decide.

Life becomes quieter—not because it is easier, but because it is clearer. Living with enough does not mean disengaging from responsibility. It means responsibility is right-sized. You participate where participation is appropriate and step back where it is not. You carry what is yours, and you allow others to carry what belongs to them.

This is not a one-time insight. It is a practice. A way of life. Some days you will misjudge. You will add more than is required or hesitate when action is needed. *Enough* allows room for correction. It does not demand perfection—only honesty.

Over time, that honesty produces something most people are chasing but cannot force: Peace.

Not the absence of effort.
Not the absence of conflict.
But the absence of unnecessary weight.

Peace is what happens when enough is rightly judged. This is what it means to live your life in the right measure. And when you do, life does not become smaller. It becomes manageable.

And that is enough.

Voices That Informed This Work

Alongside lived experience and applied clinical practice, the work presented here is informed by established clinical frameworks in attachment theory, trauma-informed care, and recovery from self-abandonment.

The voices listed below reflect influences that helped shape the perspective and approach underlying ENOUGH.

Bowlby, J. (1988). A secure base: Parent-child attachment and healthy human development. Basic Books.

Brown, B. (2012). Daring greatly: How the courage to be vulnerable transforms the way we live, love, parent, and lead. Gotham Books.

Cloud, H., & Townsend, J. (1992). Boundaries: When to say yes, how to say no to take control of your life. Zondervan.

Levine, P. A. (2010). In an unspoken voice: How the body releases trauma and restores goodness. North Atlantic Books.

Mellody, P. (1989). Facing codependence: What it is, where it comes from, how it sabotages our lives. Harper & Row.

Mellody, P., Miller, A. W., & Miller, J. K. (2003). Facing codependence: What it is, where it comes from, how it sabotages our lives (Rev. ed.). HarperOne.

Van der Kolk, B. A. (2014). The body keeps the score: Brain, mind, and body in the healing of trauma. Viking.

About the Author

Melinda Haynes is a trauma-informed licensed therapist, author, and the founder of a nonprofit serving families impacted by trauma. With lived experience and over two decades of walking alongside others in the work of healing, she writes for those who are ready to stop performing, release unnecessary weight, and live with greater clarity, integrity, and purpose. Her work invites readers to know when enough is *enough*.

www.ingramcontent.com/pod-product-compliance
Lightning Source LLC
Chambersburg PA
CBHW031508040426
42444CB00007B/1258